Amazon Echo
The Ultimate Guide to Learn Amazon Echo In No Time (Amazon Echo, Alexa Skills Kit, smart devices, digital services, digital media)

ANDREW BUTLER

CONTENTS

Introduction

Alexa is at once familiar because of her near human voice and standard answers. Did you know that her answers can be customized by design through some simple coding? It makes the possibilities of using Alexa endless!

Apple has never made Siri with 3rd party apps and her integration into their platform is a priority. However, Alexa is open to anyone. She's designed to be a full integration between developer and device. This creates a new avenue to explore the voice-driven behaviors through the Alexa Skill Kit. Amazon's approach to the technology/developer relationship is to let developers present new Skills for Alexa to learn and integrate such as:

- Allow them to write custom code for responses to questions

- Use as an interaction model
- Create prompts that Alexa will speak
- Create icons and graphics for the Alexa smartphone app
- Create key phrases that are recognized

Alexa can be programmed for many customer service situations like ticketing, parking, banking, and purchasing of specialty food products at a large grocery store. Alexa could be customized for genre-specific phrases like "How much is a ticket to the 7 o'clock movie?" or "What isle are the leche nuts in?" Banks could incorporate Alexa into an Automatic Teller where customers could ask a range of questions about their balances or transactions.

Chapter 1: Quick Start and Set Up

Before you get around to programming Echo, it is helpful to get the device set up so that you can begin to explore its functionalities.

Echo's main interface, Alexa, is a voice-assistant that represents Amazon's first foray into the smart home and home automation markets.

The 7-directional microphones and powerful speaker in Echo enable it to "listen" and play music with little tininess or distortion. After you have spoken the wake word, Alexa will respond to commands made within the range of the microphones. Commands can be used to set alarms, play media, create to-do lists for a day or date range, assist in unit conversions, or give the current weather. Control support for the Philips Hue light-changing system is available as a feature that integrates with a larger smart home scenario. The Alexa Voice Service is the driving force behind the Echo device and enables the user(s) to execute or query a variety of commands.

The Echo has three actual, tangible things you can touch on the cylinder itself: the volume ring, the action button, which will wake Alexa without using her wake word, and the microphone button, which is handy when you don't want Alexa to listen to you at all, not even for the wake word.

It is generally recommended that prior to the first use of the speakers the sound ring is turned down, as the Echo is shipped with volume at full and it can be loud. The ring is located at the top of the speaker.

Setting Up Your Echo

Before your Echo is out of the box, the Amazon Alexa App should be downloaded from the App Store. Do not launch the app immediately.

Plug the Echo in. The ring around the top should flash blue and then change to a rotating orange. At this point the Echo is ready to be configured with your Wi-Fi network. Should the ring turn purple, it would mean that you have missed the Wi-Fi configuration window and it is likely that Alexa will begin to try and tell you what to do next. Simply hold down the action button for 5 seconds and the ring should turn orange once again. If Alexa is still too loud it is a good time to turn the volume down.

During configuration mode, launch the Wi-Fi settings on your smart phone. You will see the Echo as an available connectable device—this enables direct configuration of Echo.

The Echo will be listed as something with the word Amazon in it. Connect it and then launch the Amazon Alexa app that was downloaded earlier. The Alexa app should self-initiate the configuration process; however, if it does not just tap the menu icon and select "settings" manually.

From the settings menu one of two things may be selected: "[Your Name] Echo," if you purchased the device yourself, or "Set up new device" if the Echo was a gift.

From this point, connect to the Echo directly, and with the app open, the remainder of the set up is easy. Use your Amazon login information when prompted, agree to the Alexa conditions, and connect Echo to your home Wi-Fi network. Next we will explore talking to Alexa and customizing your Echo and Alexa experience.

Chapter 2: Talking to Alexa

Echo is programmed to react to a "wake word." The default wake word is the assistant's name, Alexa. The wake word can be changed to Amazon if there is someone in your house with the name Alexa. This change can be managed in the settings menu. With the default wake word programmed, when you say the word "Alexa" the light ring at the top of the unit will spin blue and then the brightest part of the light display will orient itself to the source of the sound. As the Echo recognizes the wake word, you may then follow with a query or command.

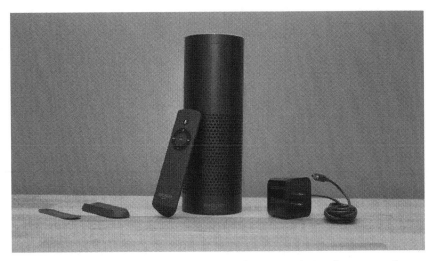

Test this by asking Alexa a simple question that you know the answer to. Note that simple does not necessarily mean easy. Out of the box, Alexa is a "teachable" unit, hence the expandable aspect of the programming. Just check to see that Alexa's mics are working properly, picking up the sound in the correct place, and is able to connect to a robust Wi-Fi in order to access the information to answer your query.

The Stop Command:

This single word may be the most important part of using Alexa. It immediately quiets Alexa if you have inadvertently produced an erroneous answer to a question, or posed a poorly worded question that causes Alexa to respond with a lot of chatter, music, or noise that was unintended. Simply say "Alexa Stop" and the senseless, noisy chatter will cease. With that command down it is now time to look at the fun things that Alexa can accomplish right after set up.

<u>Inquiries, Trivia, and Real-Time Conversions:</u>

The most popular task that Alexa is currently used for is playing music. The second most common thing done with Alexa is simply asking her questions. As stated above, Alexa is smart out of the box and her answers to a wide range of questions support this. For most answers Alexa will produce a direct response. In the case of a question that is out of the Echo database, like Siri, Alexa will produce search results from the internet to assist.

Some of the practical queries are:

Alexa, how do you spell [word]?

Alexa, what is the capital of [state or country]?

Alexa, what is the weather like in [geographical place]?

Alexa, what is 2+2? (Or any other simple math function)

Alexa, what is the news today?

Alexa, what time is it in [geographical place]?

Alexa, how many tablespoons are in a cup?

Alexa, who won the 2004 World Series?

As you can see, out of the box Alexa is prepared to assist with a wide range of tasks and queries.

One of the more entertaining things you can do with Alexa is ask her trivia questions, as we touched upon with the World

Series example question. Alexa can produce answers like, who played and won the game. She can even tell you where the game took place. However, when tasked with the question of the final score of the series or scoring for each game, she is unable to answer directly and has to resource the internet for the answer. All that being said, Alexa is *generally* able to answer most trivia questions that you ask her.

Questions along the lines of fastest land animal, how big planets are, how far they are from Earth, famous Peabody Award winners, and the Grammy for best album in 1984 were all easily and quickly answered by Alexa.

Playing Music:

Since the introduction of speakers, people have been playing music in their homes. Alexa syncs to your Amazon Prime music by default and also has access to the big and varied library of free music in the Prime database.

Like Siri, Alexa responds to a myriad of commands related to music in many different classifications:

Alexa play [band name].

Alexa play [song name] by [band name].

Alexa play [playlist name].

Alexa play [music genre].

Alexa, like Siri and Cortana, can also assist the user who wants to know what a song they are listening to is or who it is by:

Alexa what's playing?

Alexa what song is this?

Alexa who sings this song?

Simple music genre-specific commands may also be used like:

Alexa play Halloween music.

If you ask Alexa to play something more abstract like "scary music," however, she is unable to process the command. So there are some limitations to how you word your commands.

Now that Alexa is talking and responding easily to you, you may want to customize your use and environment within Alexa. This can easily be accomplished by adjusting Alexa's settings. For example, if the user really likes the Reuters News, Alexa can be made to source only from Reuters when the phrase "Alexa what's the news today?" is used.

Customization of Echo can be done by opening the Alexa app and selecting settings within the main menu. Scroll down to the "account" section and you will find options for items like music (link Echo to Spotify or Pandora for added music playing ability), sports update (where you can change teams that you follow within a sport), flash briefing (where the news source is changed), traffic updates, connected home products (like those Philips Hue lights we mentioned), and a daily, weekly, or monthly calendar preference.

NPR is the default news channel for Alexa, but if you want to change it to Reuters you would need to select "account" from your settings menu and then under "flash briefing," switch NPR off and turn Reuters on. If you want news from both sources simply turn the Reuters switch on in addition to NPR.

Echo is now set up and customized for your basic needs. With that complete you can now begin to test Alexa (invite a friend over to help), and figure out what Skills you may want to add to enhance specific usability of the service. In the following section information can be found on setting up the developer side of Echo's functionality.

Chapter 3: The Developer Portal

Working with the Developer Portal:

Creating an Alexa Skill with ASK (Alexa Skill Kit) requires that you use some specific tools and services:

1. You will need to have an active account on the Amazon Developer Portal. This is the place to configure the skill and prepare it for release.

2. It is required to have the ability to develop and deploy on a cloud-based service to an internet accessible endpoint. Simply, the service provides the interface for the processing of user questions and provides replies from the queried element (in this case, Alexa).

3. Access to a development environment that is appropriate for the language used. Language choices include Node.js, Java, or Python.

4. Hardware required for testing (in this case an Echo unit).

It is fully possible to choose the tools and services that will be used directly from Amazon, in most cases from AWS (Amazon Web Services). This is the simplest place for the beginner to start unless one is well versed in cloud technologies.

Once all tools and services have been chosen it is time to begin the Skill development in earnest.

Here is an example of a skill developed to find the best place to ski. This skill enables the user to ask Alexa the following questions:

- Where is my favorite place to ski?
- My favorite ski mountain is FGH.
- How's the snow?
- How's the snow at FGH?

This is a quick overview of the steps to create this new Skill:

1. Log in to the Amazon Developer Portal (https://developer.amazon.com/home.html) using your preferred web browser

2. Select Apps & Services.

3. Select Alexa.

4. Select Alexa Skills Kit.

5. Select Add a New Skill.

6. Give the new Skill a name (this name displays in the Alexa App on a smartphone).

7. Give the new Skill an Invocation name (this name is what users will say to interact with your Skill).

8. Designate the Endpoint URL for the new skill (this is the code Alexa uses to process the Skill).

Chapter 4: Define Voice and Process Requests

Next, the interaction model for the skill must be designed. This defines how the customer uses the Skill you have produced. This outlines the basic flow of interaction:

1. User makes a query
2. Alexa identifies the correct Skill name then sends the user request to that Skill.
3. Skill will then process the request and reply with a text response.
4. Alexa converts that text response to voice and streams to the speaker.
5. Skill may also send a graphical response for any companion app—this is optional

By definition, an Interaction Model for a Skill will have the following components:

1. Intent Schema: JSON structure that declares a set of intents (actions) the Skill can accept as well as process.
2. Sample Utterances: structured text file that connects intents to predisposed voice phrases and contains as many representative phrases as possible.

Here is a simple Intent Schema for allowing a user to set his/her favorite ski mountain. The user would do this by saying "SkiCheck, my favorite ski mountain is <resort name here>."

```
{
     "intents": [
     {
"intent": "SkiCheck",
          "slots": [
          {
               "name": "SkiMountain",
               "type": "ListOfSkiMountains"
          }
          ]
     }
     ]
}
```

The JSON above should look familiar to the coding eye. If this really makes no sense at all, fear not, here is a list of each section and its meaning:

- intents: will define all of the intents (or actions) your Skill will support
- intent: will define a specific intent with a given name (SurfCheck)
- slots: will define all of the slots (or placeholders) within an intent
- name: will define the name of the slot (SurfSpot)
- type: will define the type of the slot (ListOfSurfSpots). This could be a custom type or one of the many predefined types provided by Amazon.

Within a few lines of JSON, we have defined an intent that allows the user to set their favorite ski mountain. However, in order to make the intent clear we need to tell Alexa what phrases have interaction with this intent. We do this with the utterances.

Here are some utterances we might use for our new Skill:

SkiCheck my favorite ski mountain is [ski mountain]
SkiCheck [ski mountain]

SkiCheck what is my favorite ski mountain?

The first word in any utterance should be the name of the intent; in this example it would be SkiCheck. This directly ties these utterances back to one of the above intent definitions (there is only one, but often there are several). The second utterance is the name of the specific slot, SkiMountain. This instructs the intent to accept phrases that are solely defined in the slot definition. The slot accepts its name from the list of ski mountains, such as Vail. The intent definition (JSON) and sample utterances (text file) are both set in the Developer Portal for the skill in the Interaction Model section.

When the Interaction Model has been defined, you will then provide code that processes the requests for your Skill.

Chapter 5: Test and Certify

There are really only two parts to each Skill: the voice interface and the query processing. Initially, you request something from Alexa with your voice. Next, the request is processed by code floating in the cloud. With a defined voice interface and code developed to process requests for your Skill, all you need to do is test to make sure it works. The Developer Portal is where all the Skill's testing is done, the Lambda function section enables you to use web-based tools to test successfully. The AWS portal also allows definition of Input Test Events in the JSON format. This JSON simulates an Alexa response environment. If a user asked, "SkiCheck my favorite ski mountain is Vail," this JSON is sent to the Skill to process:

```
{
"session": {
```

```
"new": false,
"sessionId": "session1234",
"attributes": {},
"user": {
  "userId": null
},
"application": {
  "applicationId": "amzn1.echo-sdk-
ams.app.stoked-software.surf-check"
 }
},
"version": "1.0",
"request": {
  "intent": {
    "slots": {
      "SkiMountain": {
        "name": "SkiMountain",
        "value": "Vail"
      }
    },
    "name": "SkiCheck"
  },
  "type": "IntentRequest",
  "requestId": "request5678"
}
}
```

The values above match what was used for the Voice Interface and Interaction Model sections earlier in this text. Each intent supported by the Skill can be tested in this developer environment. Testing is the final step in the process before the Skill is submitted to Amazon for certification.

Submit for Certification:

Amazon provides a submission checklist to assist with the process. The Skill must follow rules that are defined by Amazon. Skills cannot solicit sensitive information or be targeted towards minors. They cannot request health or financial information and they must do what they advertise in sample utterances. If the Skill passes all the criteria set forth by Amazon, it will be made available to all Amazon Echo devices.

Chapter 6: Smart Home Skills

A Smart Home Skill (SHS) enables you to create skills that control cloud-connected devices across your Wi-Fi network. For example, you could turn off your bedroom light without leaving the haven of your warm bed.

To build a SHS you can use the Smart Home Skill API. Although this will give you less control (as a developer) over the user's experience, it will simplify the development process as you won't need to create the voice user interface. By using this process, the Smart Home Skill API will define the requests the skill can handle (known as *device directives),* and the words that users say to make these requests.

For example, a device directive could be turned on or turned off, and the words the user would say could be, "turn off the bedroom lights."

As the developer of this SHS you would define how your skills will respond to a particular device directive. Following the same example, you would write the code that makes the bedroom light turn on and off. This is called a *skill adapter.*

To build a SHS you will need the following:

- An Amazon developer account. Visit: https://developer.amazon.com/ to register for free.
- A cloud-enabled device that you want to control and use through Alexa. (In our example it would be lights.)
- An AWS (Amazon Web Service) account—this will allow you to host your skill as an AWS Lambda function.

- Foundation knowledge of OAuth 2.0.

- Basic understanding of Node.js, Java, or Python.

- An Alexa-enabled device for testing, such as the Amazon Echo, Echo Dot, or Fire TV.

How to Build a Smart Home Skill

Step 1: Create a Skill

1. Open the Amazon Developer Portal and log in > Click *Apps and Services* > Choose *Alexa* > Click *Get Started* > Choose *Add a New Skill*. This will open a page titled *Skill Information* > Select *Smart Home Skill API* > Enter the name of your skill > Click *Save* > Copy the *Application ID* to your clipboard by right clicking and selecting *Copy*. Save this in a note on your desktop.

Step 2: Create a Lambda Function

1. Create an AWS account if you do not already have one. Log into the AWS Management Console > Select AWS Lambda > In the top right-hand corner define the *Region* by choosing from the dropdown list. Note: Lambda functions for Alexa must be hosted by this region.

2. Click *Create a Lambda function* > Select *alexa-smart-home-skill-adapter* from the blueprint page. Find this blueprint quickly by typing "Home" into the filter box.

3. Set the *Event Source Type* to *Alexa Smart Home* > Add an *Application ID* from the developer portal— this was copied to your clipboard > Click *Next*.

4. Enter *Name* and *Description* for your skill. Select *Python 2.7* for the *Runtime* (You can also use Node.js or Java). > Check that *Edit Code Inline* is selected.

5. Enter the following code into the code editor.

Note: This code is only a starting point. This code determines the request type, but the response is not fully implemented. Remember that you will need to handle every type of request that a user could make to your skill and provide all the necessary responses.

- Don't change the *Handler* default name from *lambda_function.lambda_handler*. A function handler is the main entry point for a Lambda function.
  The file name in the console will be *lambda_function* and the *lambda_handler* function will be the entry point.

- Next, select *Lambda_basice_execution* from the *Role options* > Leave all of the *Advanced Settings* as they are *(set to defaults)* > Click *Next*.

- Check that all the information displayed is correct > Click *Create Function*.

- When your function has been completed a summary page will be displayed. In the top right-hand corner, copy the Amazon Resource Name (ARN). You will need this to configure the smart home skill in the developer portal.

Step 3: Register Your Skill

1. Open the Amazon Developer Portal and log in > Click *Apps and Services* > Choose *Alexa* > Select your skill from the list > Click through the *Interaction Model Tab* until you reach the page titled *Configuration* > Copy the ARN number from the Lambda function into the *Endpoint* field > Enable *Account Linking*. For this the following is required:

- Authorization URL
- Client ID
- Redirect URL
- Authorization Grant Type—for this, ensure *Authorization Code Grant is* selected.

  For Authorization Grant Type you will need to supply the following:

  > Access Token URI: (The URL for the OAuth Server)

  > Client Secret: (This is so that the Alexa service can authenticate with the Access Token URI.)

  > Client Authentication Scheme: (Identifies the type of authentication Alexa should use)

> Privacy Policy URL: (A URL for a page with your privacy policy. This link is displayed in the Alexa app and is required for smart home skills.)

2.   Choose *Yes* to enable testing.

Step 4: Test Your Skill

To test your skill you will need to use an Alexa-enabled device.

1.   Open the Lambda Console > Select your smart home skill > Click on *Event Source* Tab > Select *Alexa Smart Home* > Make sure *State* is enabled > Save > Close Lambda Console.

2.   Open the Alexa App > Click *Skills* > Enter the name of your smart home skill > Search > *Enable* and *Account-link* your skill to the device cloud it is designed to work with.

3.   Click the *Smart Home* tab on the home screen of the Alexa App > Choose *Your Devices* > Give Alexa commands using the utterances you have programmed your skill to support with the device names you've set for the devices in your account that is linked to the device cloud.

4.   Repeat Step 3 until you are satisfied.

Step 5: Submit Your Skill

1. Open the developer portal > Click on the *Alexa Section* > Choose *Get Started* > Select your smart home skill > Click *Next* until you reach *Publishing Information* > Fill in *Short Skill* and *Full Skill* descriptions. > Ensure *Category* is set to *Smart Home* > Add *Keywords* if you want > Add small and large icons as long as they meet the described guidelines > Add any testing instructions for the certification team > Click *Next* > Answer the questions about *Privacy and Compliance* > Click *Submit for Certification.*

Step 6: Maintenance

Remember that even though you have published your skill it is always advisable to keep maintaining it. Enhance features, fix bugs, and improve the overall experience.

Chapter 7: Developing Your Lambda Function Endpoint—Setting Your Environment

The first thing that needs to be done in order to set the environment for the Lambda function is to copy and paste the blueprint. Save this to a file named "index.js". This should be named exactly like the first part of the handler. Therefore, if the handler parameter is set to "index.handler" then the file needs to be named "index.js". The folder containing these files should be located on the home computer. Node.js can also be installed at this time. The link to the node.js download can be found here.

If it is necessary to install a module, open a terminal. You may do so by typing in the following in the cmd.exe window on an OSX or Windows computer:

```
////
$ cd your_directory_name
$ npm install module_name
////
```

The final instruction should install a module and will create the "node_nodule" folder in your original folder.

The Handler: the Keeper of Standard Skill Logic

After the nodule has been created it may be used in the skill code. A connection must be made before executing the remainder of the code. Like the timeout parameter, this *must* be done synchronously or the function may complete its execution prior to the connection being fully established. This is a valuable tip in order to complete other steps that may take additional time to execute, like an intensive computation or API request.

Routing the incoming instruction sent by Amazon Echo is within the first group of instructions within the exports.handler = function (event context) {" and "} group. Three major functions will be executed dependent on the received request.

Those functions are:

- <u>onSessoinStarted:</u> executes if this is a new session
- <u>onLaunch:</u> executed if there is no specific question asked. It will redirect to another response << getWelcomeResponse >>. This final function fires the standard welcome message
- <u>onIntent:</u> executed if a question recognized by the skill is asked

Each question that Alexa answers has to have a defined intent. The intent is also named in the developer portal. It can be set later.

Here is a coding example for the single question: What are the best new smart devices? This question will have a single << intent >> possibility. The intent is named "GetBestNewSmartDevices".

```
////
function onIntent(intentRequest, session, callback) {
    console.log("onIntent requestId=" +
intentRequest.requestId +
        ", sessionId=" + session.sessionId);
    var intent = intentRequest.intent,
        intentName = intentRequest.intent.name;
    // Dispatch to your skill's intent handlers
```

```
    if ("GetBestNewSmartDevices" === intentName) {
        response_to_intent_GetBestNewSmartDevices(intent,
session, callback);
    } else if ("AMAZON.HelpIntent" === intentName) {
        getWelcomeResponse(callback);
    } else {
        throw "Invalid intent";
    }
////
```

This code receives the intent name that is stored in "intentRequest.intent.name". The code will check only for the function to execute this single request. There has now been a newly defined function: response_to_intent_GetBestNewSmartDevices.

The function has the normal, standard parameters (intent, callback, and session). Within the variable intent is the word pronounced by the inquirer—if there is a question with a parameter chosen.

Below is a function that will execute on this simple intent:

```
////
function response_to_intent_GetBestNewSmartDevices
(intent, session, callback)
```

```
{
    if (no_res_GetBestNewSmartDevices || no_db_con)
    { // If the request to get the answers for the intent
GetBestNewSmartDevices has failed OR the database
connexion has failed
        var cardTitle = "Sorry, Something Wrong Occurred";
        var sessionAttributes = {};
        var repromptText = "";
        var speechOutput = "";
        var shouldEndSession = true;
        if (no_res_GetBestNewSmartDevices)
        {
            // If the request has failed or there is no result
            speechOutput = "I'm sorry the server of Anythings.co
are overloaded. Please try again later";
            speechOutput = "I'm sorry the server of Anythings.co
are overloaded. Please try again later";
        }
        else if (no_db_con)
        {
            // IF the database connection could not be made
            speechOutput = "I'm sorry the server of Anythings.co
are overloaded. Please try again later";
            speechOutput = "I'm sorry the server of Anythings.co
are overloaded. Please try again later";
        } else
```

```
    {
        speechOutput = "I'm sorry the server of Anythings.co
are overloaded. Please try again later";
        speechOutput = "I'm sorry the server of Anythings.co
are overloaded. Please try again later";
    }
        callback(sessionAttributes,
        buildSpeechletResponse(cardTitle, speechOutput,
repromptText, shouldEndSession));
    }
    else
    { // If there is no error
        var cardTitle = "Top 3 IoT Devices";
        var sessionAttributes = {};
        var repromptText="";
        var speechOutput="";
        var shouldEndSession = true;
        speechOutput = "The best three new smart devices today
are: "+product1name+", "+product1tagline+".
"+product2name+", "+product2tagline+".
"+product3name+", "+product3tagline+". See you later on
Anythings.co !";


        repromptText = "The best three new smart devices today
are: "+product1name+", "+product1tagline+".
```

"+product2name+", "+product2tagline+".
"+product3name+", "+product3tagline+". See you later on Anythings.co !";
    callback(sessionAttributes,
       buildSpeechletResponse(cardTitle, speechOutput, repromptText, shouldEndSession));
  }
}
////

It should be mentioned that these instructions have been made before the function is executed:

- Connect to the database: when successful the flag variable << no_db_con >> is set to the initial value of "false." If there is a connection error this will then be set to "true."
- Make the request: when successful the flag variable << no_res_GetBestNewSmartDevices >> is set to the initial value of "false." When there is an error or no results are yielded, this will be set to "true."

An answer in every case is determined by the defined flag, even if there is no connection or no results to the request.

In either case, at the end some variables will need to be

defined:

- cardTitle: this is the title that is displayed on the Alexa app
- repromptText: this will be used in case of user error in response to a question or if the user does not answer
- speechOutput: this is what Alexa processes as a response
- shouldEndSession: this is a boolean attribute that helps to define if a skill should end or if it should interact with the user an additional time. If this is set to false the skill will end.

This is where error messages are set, so that if something wrong occurs, dynamic text should be constructed in the speechOutput variable.

Amazon defines some useful tips within this blueprint, like the buildSpeechletResponse function, for example. Amazon blueprints are very well coded so there will only have to be slight modifications for individual functionality:

1. Add the intent on the onIntent function
2. Specific functions for each intent will send the text that is to be read to the user

3. modification of the getWelcomeResponse function defines the message served if no intent is made.

When the code is ready, zip it with the node_nodule folder and upload the coding through the AWS Lambda screen. Now configurations have to be made to the interaction model so that the function works.

Return to the Alexa Configuration Screen

Paste the reference to the Lambda that was just created onto the endpoint input. The reference starts with arn:aws:lambda:us-east-XXXXX. This can be found in the right corner of the Lambda configuration screen. Amazon's terminology refers to this as the << ARN >>. Select the "next" button to define the interaction model. Intent Schema is a JSON-like variable which describes all intents and gives each a unique name. These names are transferred to the Lambda function to ensure processing of the request.

Below is an example of this based on prior coding:

```
{
  "intents": [
    {
      "intent": "GetWhatWorksWith",
      "slots": [
```

```
    {
      "name": "Product",
      "type": "LIST_OF_PRODUCTS"
    }
   ]
  },
  {
    "intent": "GetBestNewSmartDevices"
  }
 ]
}
```

For this function there are two defined intents: GetWhatWorkWith and GetBestNewSmartDevices. The latter is easier as there is no slot or parameter. This means the question that is asked contains no content that needs to be transmitted to the code in order to make the correct answer.

The second has a single << slot >> because the question that is posed contains a parameter that must be transmitted. Here the custom slot type is defined as << LIST_OF_PRODUCTS >> this also must have a name. Defining custom slots is done by simply selecting the "add slot type" button and copy and pasting the chosen name. Enter the product values, separated by line breaks, that will be recognized and passed to the coding. For this skill it is a list of products.

Sample Utterances will then need to be defined. These are listed as sample questions that assist the Amazon algorithm in recognizing which questions match what intents. For the skill referred to in the code above these are:

GetBestNewSmartDevices: what the best smart devices are
GetWhatWorksWith: what works with [product]

Note that it is not necessary to punctuate these text strings. The system must be written so that in the second part of the question it will contain the variable parameter of what pairs with [product]. The [product] is the parameter in this case. Alexa recognizes this and will attempt to match what is said in the query with the list that is held in the custom slot type, then Alexa will pass it. If there is no available match this will be passed "as is" to the coding.

Chapter 8: Amazon Echo and Echo Dot

<u>A Quick Overview of Amazon Echo:</u>

At its core the Amazon Echo is a wireless speaker that happens to be smart as well. However, this simple explanation does not fully capture the potential of this twenty-first-century device. It isn't just a personal assistant, but with the wide range of functionality Echo possesses, it will feel like you have your own digital assistant right there for every need and want to make life easier.

What really sets Echo apart from devices like Siri and Cortana is the ability to recognize and process voice commands through the Alexa OS and outside a smartphone device. Alexa's functionality is furthered by its omnidirectional speakers and microphones, which mean that it can be activated from anywhere that Alexa can hear you. After the voice recognition has been trained over time it will understand individual users even with an uncommon dialect or accent.

Amazon Echo Dot:

This is the Mini-me of the Echo cylinder. Dot comes with a basic speaker which allows it to function in a smaller and lighter format. Dot has the ability to connect with a user's own wired or wireless speakers, something that is currently impossible with the full-sized Echo. Dot enables the user to connect Bluetooth or 3.5mm plug speakers. Dot offers much of what the full size Echo does and is powered by the exact same Alexa-based voice-recognition system.

Some of the functionality of Dot is the ability to place orders on Amazon, get current news and weather, stream music or live media, and full integration with smart home products like Nest Thermostat.

Along with the smaller size, the price on the Echo Dot is

about half of that of the full-sized model. Dot is perfect for those who may want an Echo in every room of the house. Set one as a wake up alarm and another in the kitchen to control the smart appliances, use one in the gym to stream music during a workout, and ask for today's weather in the living room before heading out for the day.

Echo Dot is only available through Alexa Voice shopping and limited to Amazon Prime customers who already have an Echo device or Alexa-enabled Amazon Fire TV. It is assumed that as integration continues with the Dot and Echo products, some of these limitations will be lifted over time.

So, which Echo device is best suited to the currents needs of the customer? That is up to the user to decide. The full size Echo is great for use in one room of the house to complete simple or complex tasks or queries when most users will interact with Echo in a single space.

Echo Dot offers much of the same functionality in a smaller format. The speaker is basic and will sound as such when streaming music. Dot is a much more portable version of the Echo and can be easily moved from room to room or kept in every room of the house.

Chapter 9: Amazon Tap

One of the most common complaints about the full-sized Amazon Echo is that it has too many features and is cost prohibitive to some people. If Echo was made to execute less functions and had a smaller size it would have more of a mass appeal. Enter Amazon Tap.

<u>Amazon Tap:</u>

The Tap is a more portable and simple version of the full-sized Echo. At about two-thirds the size of the full unit it can be placed almost anywhere and moved from place to place with ease. The power source of Tap is also different than the full-sized unit; the Tap is battery-powered and not able to plug into an outlet. This feature also enhances the mobility of the unit. The battery life is about 9 hours for Tap when it is doing something continuous like streaming music or some other media. The unit will last 3 weeks when in standby mode.

The name Tap comes from the way the device interaction is initiated. Unlike Echo, Tap does not have a voice-activated wake word. You must press or "tap" the unit's button in order to ready it for a command. This may seem a bit inconvenient, but on the plus side, with Tap it does not feel like the unit is "spying" on you by listening to your every word and conversation within its microphone's "earshot."

Tap answers questions and streams music through Alexa, just like the full-sized Echo unit, but also possesses the unique feature of being able to connect to all mobile devices through Bluetooth and can stream music directly from devices in this way. Tap can be turned into a portable speaker to stream music and media on the go.

Still stuck between the Echo and Tap devices? Here are some main, basic differences that may help with your decision:

- Echo is great for those users who would like a stationary unit, in one space, to perform a myriad of simple or advanced tasks.
- Tap is meant for the user that needs simpler functionality on the go and want to use their unit in

tandem with other devices to stream music from those devices, like a smartphone.

With such simple and defined differences, the choice for you should be clear. But Amazon has a wide range of products that allows it to be paired with Echo and Alexa interfaces. Start with what is affordable for you and go from there. As your home becomes more and more integrated with smart products, the need for Echo and Tap will become part of the home experience. The Nest Thermostat is a great place to start and will become an instant favorite as it cuts home heating bills. Devices that answer the door or activate appliances remotely are also currently available for use with Alexa products.

Chapter 10: SMART Technology

The Amazon Echo device is capable of controlling compatible smart appliances within the household. This includes lights, switches, heaters, and many more. The Alexa app allows you to group all smart devices for easier and more efficient management. For instance, you can group all smart lights in the kitchen in a single group. This way, you only need to say the group name in your voice command instead of separating each device into multiple commands.

The list of compatible smart products continues to grow. This chapter will only include the most common products used with the Amazon Echo. Some smart technology requires "Skills" and this will be discussed in the next chapter.

Philips Hue

Hue bulbs are one of the smart products under the Philips brand. The brightness of these bulbs can be controlled and the light colors can be changed too. Linking these devices to the Echo speaker allows users to control the Philips Hue bulbs through voice commands.

Make sure that all Hue bulbs are connected to the same Wi-Fi network. Go to the Alexa app and search for the bulbs. Refer to the Philips user guide for how to connect the Philips Hue to your Wi-Fi network. After successfully pairing the bulbs with the Echo, you can now manage the lights with these commands:

Alexa, dim the lights to 50 percent.
Alexa, turn off the lights.

If you grouped the lights, then you can use the following format for your voice command:

Alexa, switch on [group name].

SmartThings

Smart products under the SmartThings label are also compatible with the Echo device. This ranges from lights, power outlets, and switches. The SmartThings power outlets allow you to control any device or appliances that are plugged in. This means that you can also control non-smart appliances using the Amazon Echo via SmartThings power outlets.

Link the SmartThings device to the Amazon Echo through the Alexa app. Go to Settings and look for "Connected Home." You will be able to link the smart devices from there. The voice commands that you can use are similar to the Philips Hue voice commands.

Wink

Wink hub, similar to SmartThings, powers outlets and functions as a central device to help you manage Wink-compatible devices. Here is the list of devices that are currently compatible with both Wink hub and Amazon Echo.

- Commercial Electric
  o Smart LED Downlight
- Cree

- o Connected LED Bulb
- EcoSmart
  - o Smart A19
  - o Smart PAR20
  - o Smart GU10
  - o Smart BR30
- GE
  - o Link A19
  - o Link BR30
  - o Link PAR38
- Leviton
  - o Z-wave Scene Capable Dimmer
  - o Z-wave Scene Capable Switch
  - o Z-wave Scene Capable Receptacle
  - o Z-wave Scene Capable Plug-In Module
  - o Z-wave Scene Capable Plug-In Appliance Module
- Lutron
  - o Caseta Plug-On Lamp Dimmer
  - o Caseta In-Wall Dimmer
- Osram
  - o Lightly White-tunable Smart LED Bulb
- Philips
  - o Hue A19
  - o Hue BR30
- TCP

o A19 Bulb

Insteon

Aside from SmartThings and Wink, Amazon Echo is also compatible with Insteon hub. You can also control all the devices plugged in the Insteon hub. As of the writing of this book, the only compatible Insteon hub so far is the Hub 2245 – 222. Pairing this hub to the Alexa app will allow you to use the Echo device in triggering connected appliances and lights.

WeMo

Users of WeMo devices can also pair them with the Amazon Echo. The Echo speaker will automatically detect the WeMo device if it is connected to the same Wi-Fi network. As of today, the only WeMo devices compatible with the Amazon Echo are the following:

- WeMo Switch
- WeMo Light Switch
- WeMo Insight

Connect these devices to the Wi-Fi network using the WeMo app and the Amazon Echo will automatically detect them.

The voice commands that you can use are similar to that of the Philips Hue voice commands.

Chapter 11: Defining Utterances

Examples for request phrases for Amazon Echo skills are a must when developing so users have a guide to show them how to best utilize the skill. The more examples that are provided, the more useful Echo can be, but it's also a lot more work. Call it a labor of love. Echo Utterance Expander has been designed to assist the programmer with this task. Amazon apps or Skills have one or more functions or features—these are the Skill's "intents." Asking questions or giving a command is how the user activates the intents within an Alexa Skill. With the richness of the English language there are often more ways than one to pose a query or command. The Queries or commands that activate intents within Alexa are called Utterances. Many Utterances can be used for activation of one's intent.

The Amazon guidelines recommend samples for all Utterances that are possible to invoke a specific intent. There is a 30 example list that Amazon also provides to assist programmers in beginning an Utterance.

The function of the app may dictate that information from the Utterances that are necessary for the Skill's execution. This could mean that the list of Utterances is limited and predictable, like weather and concert times and sometimes there is so much available information that only a small part is used in the Utterances. Less predictable Utterances could be names of one hit wonders, or fatalities in the Civil War. Utterances are defined by what Amazon calls Slots, which are much like a fill-in-the-blank system.

With Slots that accept infinite values, Amazon directs the programmer to give answers for all possible Slot values. A Skill that supports MLB game schedules might also support a query of when a team's next home game is.

Using only one way of making the query, the Utterances would include:

When is the next Rockies game?

When is the next Angels game?

When is the next Cubs game?

... and so on for all MLB teams.

With just these three phrasings:

When is the next Rockies game?

When do the Rockies play next?

What is the next Rockies game?

And each phrasing had 8 small variations:

When is the next Rockies game?

When's the next Rockies game?

When is the next Rockies hockey game?

When's the next Rockies baseball game?

When is the Rockies game?

When's the Rockies game?

When is the Rockies baseball game?

When's the Rockies baseball game?

If the above were parameters for this question then the number of Utterances needed to process the question is 720 (30 x 3 x 8). It can become overwhelming to think about all the subtle differences that could cause a question to be looked at differently by the Alexa system such as the words "it is" versus "it's," for example. In the spoken language these words are interchanged easily, but in programming a Skill samples need to be written for each of these in order for the Skill to be processed correctly. This can lead to the generation of literally thousands of Utterances.

Manage Utterance Variations More Intelligently:
In the above example the most obvious thing is the repetition of words, especially the team names. The Amazon Utterance Expander tool takes care of this for the developer allowing more efficiency and breadth in the phrases. Above, eight variations were used. But, with the Expander tool the only phrase that needs to be written is:
(when is/when's) the (/next) Rockies (/baseball) game?
Now this single phrase will generate the complete list of the eight above variations. The key is easy syntax. When multiple variations are needed for phrases and/or words, one just needs to put all alternatives within a set a parentheses, separating the words with slashes. There is a may/may not alternative too, which is to leave one variation as blank. In this case:
(/please) tell me a (/funny) joke
is expanded to be:

Please tell me a funny joke
Please tell me a joke

Tell me a funny joke

Tell me a joke

Nested Variations:

Nested sets of alternatives are a legal inclusion with Expander. For example, the phrase Tell me a (story/(/funny) joke) is expanded to:

Tell me a funny joke

Tell me a joke

Tell me a story

Handling Slots-Alternatives to Slot Examples:

What date is next {(Sunday/Monday/Tuesday/Wednesday/Thursday/Friday/Saturday)|dayofweek}?

What date is next {Friday|dayofweek}?

What date is next {Monday|dayofweek}?

What date is next {Saturday|dayofweek}?

What date is next {Sunday|dayofweek}?

What date is next {Thursday|dayofweek}?

What date is next {Tuesday|dayofweek}?

What date is next {Wednesday|dayofweek}?

Utterances, Intents, and Multi-Phrasings:

All Utterances need to be preceded by the Intent name they

are paired with when samples are provided to the Amazon Developer Console. All of the Intents' Utterances are merged into a single field that is pasted on to the ADC form. Include the Intent name at the start of each Utterance that is being inputted to the Utterance Expander. Some Intents can be expressed with multiple phrases that are more complex than simple, small word variations.

Below is an example of a double Intent app that has been cut down and input to the Utterance Expander.

NextHockeyGameForTeam when is the next {(Sharks/Rangers/Red Wings)|team} game? NextHockeyGameForTeam when do the {(Sharks/Rangers/Red Wings)|team} play (/next)? NextTelevisedHockeyGame when is the next (/hockey) game on (t. v./television)?

Chapter 12: Creating a Skill in 3 Hours

The Ideation: Dad Jokes!
An Alexa Skills Kit app, Dad Jokes, is to be used either from
the Echo hardware or from a standalone or mobile device
installed with the correct software. While entertaining, this is
not the most useful app and it is more for the purpose of
displaying an easy and simple format to see more advanced
examples of coding for ASK.

The process shown will get the programmer to a point of
rough implementation with their app, therefore databases or
session persistence will not be covered. Although the
Ideation phase has been largely skipped, defining the
architecture of the Skill is a necessary step.

Architecture:
Calling upon a previous experience in the field of ASK is

useful, however if prior introduction to ASK has not been made there are many samples and code strings available in the Amazon libraries. Hosting of the app is necessary and most enhanced services will have space available for this. Node.js is the implementation that will be used for the server. It runs quickly and well and is supported by most hosts. Alexa-App Node.js generates ASK intents, utterances, and schemas easily and also saves a lot of coding time.

Implementation:

For the implementation of "Dad Jokes" Heroku was used. The Heroku dashboard initiated an empty GIT repository on the local device.

Node.js Installation:

Below is a basic Node.js installation with the needed modules:

```
Procfile
web: node index.js
package.json
{
 "name": "hey-dad",
 "version": "0.1.2",
 "dependencies": {
   "alexa-app": "2.2.x",
   "ejs": "^2.3.1",
```

```
  "body-parser": "^1.13.1",
  "express": "^4.13.0"
},
 "engines": {
  "node": "0.10.x",
  "npm": "1.2.x"
 }
}
```

Index.js Set Up

Set up the index.js file, which handles all the intents and serve jokes.

index.js
```
//initialize express
var express = require('express');
//initialize alexa-app
var alexa = require('alexa-app');
//initialize body-parser
var bodyParser = require('body-parser');
//initialize the app and set the port
var app = express();
app.set('port', (process.env.PORT || 5000));
app.use(express.static('public'));
app.use(bodyParser.urlencoded({ extended: true }));
app.use(bodyParser.json());
app.set('view engine','ejs');
```

//create and assign our Alexa App instance to an address on express, in this case https://hey-dad.herokuapp.com/api/hey-dad
var alexaApp = new alexa.app('hey-dad');
alexaApp.express(app, "/api/");

//make sure we're listening on the assigned port
app.listen(app.get('port'), function() {
    console.log("Node app is running at localhost:" + app.get('port'));
});

Alexa-App Framework and Intents
Start adding the Alexa-App framework and intents.

index.js
//our intent that is launched when "Hey Alexa, open Hey Dad" command is made
alexaApp.launch(function(request,response) {
//log our app launch
console.log("App launched");
//this is what the Alexa device will say at first
response.say("Hey champ! Do you want to hear a joke?");
//this is what it'll say when prompted again
response.shouldEndSession(false, "Come on, say: 'Tell me a

joke!'");

//send the response back to Alexa Skills to transmit to the user

response.send();

});

... (GIT for full project:<u>here</u>)

Schema and Utterances

An addition of a few pages that will display the schema and utterances for a quick copy-paste is shown below:

index.js

app.get('/schema', function(request, response) {

response.send('<pre>'+alexaApp.schema()+'</pre>');

});

app.get('/utterances', function(request, response) {

response.send('<pre>'+alexaApp.uterances()+'</pre>');

});

Amazon Skill:

To set up the Skill, copy and paste the /utterances and /schema pages to the correct places in the Amazon dashboard. In the current state it will be necessary to add intents beyond the launch intent already used to test. Set the SSL Certificate for Heroku to: "My development endpoint is a subdomain of a domain that has a wildcard certificate from a certificate authority."

<u>Schema:</u>

```
{
  "intents": []
}
```

<u>Add Intents:</u>

Adding more intents will depend greatly on the app being made. The example that has been used above is a good boilerplate that can be reused between applications. The finished application can be found <u>here</u>.

<u>Final thoughts on Alexa for Dad Jokes:</u>

ASK is a moderately powerful platform that is not a lot of work to get up and running. Third party handling of the intent recognition is a huge boon to ASK. It supports wildcards and generally matches speech instead of looking for exact, literal matches. This implementation for Dad Jokes is a simple project with no other structures. This can be expanded to any Node.js or other platform project giving a value-add to defined, pre-existing services or products. This is mainly true for data that is generally delivered as text like: house automation, interpersonal communication, etc. ASK is a reasonable platform in a market where no one provider has the lion's share.

Chapter 13: Alexa App Development for Amazon Echo Using .NET on Windows

App Development for Amazon Echo, known as Alexa skills, raises its own set of unique attributes for development for Android or iOS smartphones and devices. One of the biggest differences is that Alexa skills are not installed on the actual device. Alternatively, Alexa Skills are web-hosted on the cloud. Alexa originates from the cloud all requests that are made and then sent to the Alexa cloud-based service. The app that facilitates that request is then selected for a response which Alexa waits for and then responds verbally to the user.

Toolkits are available for various web service frameworks and languages to make development of the app easier. With toolkits the programmer does not need to produce the boilerplate code that verifies the authenticity of the requests, parses request objects, and serializes the response.

Amazon's documentation prioritizes a Linux + Java shop and teaches you how to develop using that platform.

<u>Set up the Development Environment:</u>
App endpoints are strict within the Alexa Service. Alexa will only use HTTPS on port 443 to call out, even if the app is still in the developmental phase or has been put into production by Amazon. Set up the machine being used for development to accept incoming requests on port 443 which is atypical in the development environment. Setup can sometimes be complicated if the Alexa HTTPS client that places the outbound calls to the app does not support SNI. The app needs to be *the* HTTPS endpoint bound to the host IP address—this does exclude some cloud hosting options for apps. Use of a specific web server on your development machine (IIS, IIS Express, etc.) is not necessary for incoming HTTPS traffic on Windows to be received by HTTP.SYS, a kernel-mode driver as well as a core part of the OS that passes the request to the web server. Configure HTTP.SYS to accept requests on 443. From an elevated command prompt, run
netsh http add urlacl url=https://localhost:443/
user=Everyone
Tell windows firewall to allow incoming traffic on port 443

```
netsh advfirewall firewall add rule name="HTTPS" dir=in
action=allow protocol=TCP localport=443
```

Along with receiving HTTPS traffic it is necessary to configure a development endpoint with an SSL certificate. Alexa's service validates the SSL certificate developers get from an approved CA or a generated one and registers the public key in the Amazon Developer Console. The command to self-generate a cert is

```
:makecert -r -pe -n "CN=localhost" -b 01/01/2000 -e
01/01/2036 -eku 1.3.6.1.5.5.7.3.1 -ss my -sr localMachine -
sky exchange -sp "Microsoft RSA SChannel Cryptographic
Provider" -sy 12
```

Tell HTTP.SYS which SSL certificate is being used for the development endpoint. From an elevated command prompt, run:

```
netsh http add sslcert ipport=0.0.0.0:443 appid={00112233-
4455-6677-8899-AABBCCDDEEFF} certhash=[certificate
hash]
```

Get the <certificate hash> by finding the certificate in the Certificate Manager. Run MMC.exe, go to *File | Add/Remove Snap In*, select *Certificates*. Pick the *Computer Account* and look under *Personal Certificates*. Double click on the certificate being used; you can differentiate by expiration date if there are multiple certificates. Go to *Details,* scroll down to *Thumbprint,* copy and paste the information into Notepad and remove the inner spaces before pasting it on the command line. When self-generating a cert, Amazon requires submission of its public key in the Amazon Developer Console where the Alexa app is registered, so it can be validated by the Alexa service. Alexa needs a Base 64 format for the public key called PEM in Linux and MacOS, but which Windows refers to as Base 64 encoded CER format. To certify in this format Run MMC.exe, go to *File | Add/Remove Snap In,* then select *Certificates.* Select the *Computer Account,* look under *Personal Certificates,* right click your certificate and choose Export. Choose "No, do not export the private key" and then "Base 64 encoded X.509 (.CER)" in the export wizard. Paste the content of the resulting file in the Amazon Developer Console under the app's registration, and be sure to include the BEGIN/END CERTIFICATE markers.

When done developing the Alexa app undo all this with:

netsh http delete sslcert ipport=0.0.0.0:443
netsh http delete urlacl url=https://localhost:443/

It is recommended that developers get HTTPS inbound traffic from the edge of the network to the development machine. From home this means configuring a broadband modem to send traffic coming in on 443 to the development machine. On a formal corporate network work with the network admin to set up the development machine as host in the DMZ, and if that is forbidden by policy do development on a rented VM in the cloud.

Start Developing:

Any number of web service frameworks are available to write apps. Popular ones are ASP.NET Web API or ServiceStack. Regardless of the framework that is used, the AlexaAppKit.NET toolkit makes it easy to write apps:

- It parses requests into the object model which is easily used.
- It verifies the authenticity of the request by validating signature and timestamp
- It performs automatic session and conversation managements to easily write conversational apps

Here are the high-level steps regardless of framework used:

1. **Implement ISpeechletAsync or ISpeechlet in a class that represents your app**

public interface ISpeechletAsync

```
{
    Task<SpeechletResponse> OnIntentAsync(IntentRequest
intentRequest, Session session);
    Task<SpeechletResponse>
OnLaunchAsync(LaunchRequest launchRequest, Session
session);
    Task OnSessionStartedAsync(SessionStartedRequest
sessionStartedRequest, Session session);
    Task OnSessionEndedAsync(SessionEndedRequest
sessionEndedRequest, Session session);
}
```

2. **ISpeechletAsync is recommended if the app does make requests to other cloud services**

```
public interface ISpeechlet
{
    SpeechletResponse OnIntent(IntentRequest
intentRequest, Session session);
    SpeechletResponse OnLaunch(LaunchRequest
launchRequest, Session session);
    void OnSessionStarted(SessionStartedRequest
sessionStartedRequest, Session session);
    void OnSessionEnded(SessionEndedRequest
sessionEndedRequest, Session session);
}
```

3. **Route requests from the web server hosting environment to the class**

Using ASP.NET Web API, write a small wrapper API
method:

```
public class AlexaController : ApiController
{
  [Route("my-app-endpoint")]
  [HttpPost]
  public async Task<HttpResponseMessage>
MyAppEndpoint() {
    var speechlet = new MySpeechlet();
    return await speechlet.GetResponseAsync(Request);
  }
}
```

4. **Develop, Test, Debug; Spin and Repeat**

See the raw request and response by attaching a debugger as
AlexAppKit.NET will output headers and body to the
debugger output. Fiddler should not be used as a reverse
proxy to inspect traffic from Alexa. The reason for this is
simple, when Fiddler acts a reverse proxy, it's an open proxy
and a vector for malware.

Chapter 14: Node Module Installation, Features, and API

Installation

npm install alexa-app --save

alexa-app-server Container

The alexa-app-server module uses Node.js and Express as a fully-working container for multiple alexa-app skills. Run and debug apps locally, and use as a full production server for apps.

Summary

alexa-app interprets the JSON request from Amazon, builds a JSON response, and provides convenient methods to more easily built responses, handle session objects, and add cards.

It also easily runs multiple endpoints (apps) on one Node.js server instance.

After the application's behavior has been defined, the caller (Express, Lambda,
etc.) calls the app.request() method, and passes the Alexa JSON request
object. A promise containing the response JSON is the return. The caller
then inserts that into the response, in any form it may take.

Intent schema definition and sample utterances included in your application's definition, makes it easy to generate at least hundreds of sample utterances with a small number of lines.

It should be noted that an alexa-app does not make assumptions about the context that it is running in. This runs in a stand-alone Node.js app, inside an HTTPS server, inside an AWS Lambda function, etc. The primary concern is JSON in and JSON out. There is neutral concern about the environment it is being used in, but it provides some convenient methods that will hook into some common environments.

In addition it should also be noted that if AWS Lambda is not used and you are hosting an Alexa skill on a home-based web server, users will need to validate that the requests actually come from Alexa. Validation is not provided by this module. Go here for more details on how to handle Alexa request validation, and look at who provides the necessary code, along with examples showing the process to integrate with Express.

Features

- Simplified handling of requests and generation of responses
- Asynchronous handlers are supported
- Easy connection to AWS Lambda or Node.js express; and can be connected to any other server
- Auto-generation for intent schema and sample utterances
- Easiest handling of session data
- Apps can be tested and not run on a server

Example Usage

For sample implementations use the example directory.

```
var alexa = require('alexa-app');
```

```
var app = new alexa.app('sample');
```

```
app.intent('number',

  {

    "slots":{"number":"NUMBER"}

      ,"utterances":[ "say the number {1-100|number}" ]

  },

  function(request,response) {

    var number = request.slot('number');

    response.say("You asked for the number "+number);

  }

);
```

```
// Manually hook the handler function into express
```

```
express.post('/sample',function(req,res) {

  app.request(req.body)      // connect express to alexa-app

    .then(function(response) { // alexa-app returns a promise
with the
response

    res.json(response);    // stream it to express' output

  });

});
```

API

Skills have defined handlers for functions like launch, intent, and session end, just like usual Alexa development. Alexa-app module provides a layer above this functionality to simplify this interaction. Every handler is passed a request and response object; these are custom objects for this module.

Chapter 15: Node Module Request and Response

Request

// Return the type of request received (LaunchRequest, IntentRequest, SessionEndedRequest)

String request.type()

// Return the value passed in for a given slot name

String request.slot('slotName')

// Return the value of a session variable

String request.session('attributeName')

// Session details, as passed by Amazon in the request

request.sessionDetails = { ... }

// The raw request JSON object

request.data

Response

A response JSON object will be automatically produced for the Skill. All that needs to be defined is what output is wanted.

// Tell Alexa to say something. Multiple calls to say() will be appended to
each other.

// All text output is treated as SSML

response.say(String phrase)

// Empty the response text

response.clear()

// Tell Alexa to re-prompt the user for a response, if it didn't hear
anything valid

response.reprompt(String phrase)

// Return a card to the user's Echo app

// For Object definition @see
https://developer.amazon.com/public/solutions/alexa/alexa-skills-kit/docs/al
exa-skills-kit-interface-reference#card-object

// Skill supports card(String title, String content) for
backwards compat of

type "Simple"

response.card(Object card)

// Return a card instructing the user how to link their account to the
skill.

// This internally sets the card response.

response.linkAccount()

// Tell Alexa whether the user's session is over. By default, sessions end.

// You can optionally pass a reprompt message

response.shouldEndSession(boolean end [, String reprompt])

```
// Set a session variable

// By default, Alexa only persists session variables to the
next request.
The Alex-app module

// makes session variables persist across multiple requests.

response.session(String attributeName, String
attributeValue)
```

```
// Send the response as success

// You don't usually need to call this. This is only required if
your
handler is

// asynchronous - for example, if it makes an http request
and needs to wait
for

// the response, then send it back to Alexa when finished.

response.send()
```

// Trigger a response failure

// The internal promise containing the response will be rejected, and should
be handled by

// the calling environment. Instead of the Alexa response being returned,
the failure

// message will be passed.

response.fail(String message)

// Calls to response can be chained together

response.say("OK").send();

Request Handlers

An Alexa Skill can define a single handler for the Launch event and the SessionEnded event, as well as multiple Intent handlers.

LaunchRequest

```
app.launch(function(request,response) {

  response.say("Hello World");

  response.card("Hello World","This is an example card");

});
```

IntentRequest

Use multiple calls to intent(), to Define the handler for multiple intents.

Intent handlers that do not return immediate responses (due to asynchronous operation) will return false. See example below.

Intent schema and sample utterances can be passed to intent() as well, and is detailed below.

```
app.intent('buy', function(request,response) {
```

```
    response.say("You bought a "+request.slot("item"));

});

app.intent('sell', function(request,response) {

    response.say("You sold your items!");

});
```

SessionEndRequest

```
app.sessionEnded(function(request,response) {

    // Clean up the user's server-side stuff, if necessary

    logout( request.userId );

    // No response necessary

});
```

Chapter 16: Node Module Code Execution, Schema, and Slots

Execute Code On Every Request

Programmers can define functions that will run on every request as well as define specific event handlers.

pre()

This will be executed before any event handlers. It is helpful to set up new sessions, validate the applicationId, or do other validations.

app.pre = function(request,response,type) {

    if

(request.sessionDetails.application.applicationId!="amzn1.e

```
cho-sdk-ams.app.o
ooooo-doed-oooo-adoo-oooooodooebe") {

        // Fail ungracefully

        response.fail("Invalid applicationId");

    }

};
```

It should be noted that the post() method is still called, even if the pre() function calls
send() or fail(). Post method always overrides anything done prior.

<u>post()</u>

Should be the last thing executed for each request. It is called if there is an exception or if a response was already sent. The post() function will change anything about the response and turn a response.fail() into a respond.send() with entirely new content. If post() is called after an exception is thrown, that exception is the last argument.

```
app.post = function(request,response,type,exception) {
```

// Always turn an exception into a successful response

response.clear().say("An error occurred: "+exception).send();

};

Schema and Utterances

alexa-app makes intent schema easy to define and generates many sample utterances. It is also possible to pass schema definition along with intent handlers, and extract generated content using the schema() and utterances() functions in the Skill.

Schema Syntax

Pass an object with two properties: utterances & slots

```
app.intent('sampleIntent',

    {

        "slots":{"NAME":"LITERAL","AGE":"NUMBER"},

        "utterances":[ "my {name is|name's}
```

{names|NAME} and {I
am|I'm} {1-100|AGE}{ years old|}"]

```
    },

    function(request,response) { ... }

);
```

Slots

The slots object is Name:Type mapping. The type must be one of Amazon's supported slot types: LITERAL, NUMBER, DATE, TIME, or DURATION.

Custom Slot Types

Custom slot types have this syntax:

```
app.intent('sampleIntent',

    {

        "slots":{"CustomSlotName": "CustomSlotType" },

        "utterances":[ "airport {information|status} for
{-|CustomSlotName}" ]
```

```
},

    function(request,response) { ... }

);
```

The results are an utterance list:

sampleIntent   airport information for {CustomSlotName}

sampleIntent   airport status for {CustomSlotName}

It should be noted that the "CustomSlotType" type values have to be specified within the Skill Interface's Interaction Model for a custom slot type to function correctly.

Utterances

Utterances syntax allows the generation of many (hundreds or thousands of) sample utterances (words or phrases) using some examples that get auto-expanded. Infinite sample utterances may be passed through the utterances array. Below are sample utterances and their expansion.

Multiple Options mapped to a Slot

"my favorite color is {red|green|blue|NAME}"

=>

"my favorite color is {red|NAME}"

"my favorite color is {green|NAME}"

"my favorite color is {blue|NAME}"

<u>Generate Multiple Versions of Static Text</u>
Defines multiple ways to say a phrase, combined into one
sample utterance.

"{what is the|what's the|check the} status"

=>

"what is the status"

"what's the status"

"check the status"

Auto-Generated Number Ranges

It is helpful to generate more than one sample utterance containing different numeric values when capturing a numeric slot value.

"buy {2-5|NUMBER} items"

=>

"buy {two|NUMBER} items"

"buy {three|NUMBER} items"

"buy {four|NUMBER} items"

"buy {five|NUMBER} items"

Number ranges can also increment in steps

"buy {5-20 by 5|NUMBER} items"

=>

"buy {five|NUMBER} items"

"buy {ten|NUMBER} items"

"buy {fifteen|NUMBER} items"very handler is passed
a request and response object, these are custom objects for
this module."

"buy {twenty|NUMBER} items"

Optional Words

"what is your {favorite |}color"

=>

"what is your color"

"what is your favorite color"

Using a Dictionary
Use the app's dictionary. It is possible that many intents use
the same list of possible values. Define them in a single
place, not in every intent schema.

app.dictionary = {"colors":["red","green","blue"]};

...

"my favorite color is {colors|FAVEORITE_COLOR}"

"I like {colors|COLOR}"

Generating Schema and Utterances Output

Call the schema() and utterances() functions to get the generated content out of a Skill. See examples/express.js for one way to output the data.

```
// Returns a String representation of the JSON object

app.schema() =>



{

  "intents": [

    {

      "intent": "MyColorIsIntent",

      "slots": [

        {
```

```
      "name": "Color",

      "type": "LITERAL"

    }

  ]

 }

]

}
```

app.utterances() =>

MyColorIsIntent my color is {dark brown|Color}

MyColorIsIntent my color is {green|Color}

MyColorIsIntent my favorite color is {red|Color}

MyColorIsIntent my favorite color is {navy blue|Color}

WhatsMyColorIntent whats my color

WhatsMyColorIntent what is my color

WhatsMyColorIntent say my color

WhatsMyColorIntent tell me my color

WhatsMyColorIntent whats my favorite color

WhatsMyColorIntent what is my favorite color

WhatsMyColorIntent say my favorite color

WhatsMyColorIntent tell me my favorite color

WhatsMyColorIntent tell me what my favorite color is

Cards

"Home Cards" can be sent on the Alexa app with a response.card. The companion app is available for Fire OS, Android, iOS, and desktop web browsers.

The full specification for the card object passed to this method can be found here.
Cards do not support SSML.

It should be noted that to display a card that presents the user to link their account, you should call response.linkAccount() as a shortcut.

Card Examples:
Display text only:

```
response.card({

  type:   "Simple",

  title:  "My Cool Card",  //this is not required for type Simple

  content: "This is the\ncontent of my card"

});
```

Standard aka Display text and image:
It should be noted to: Read the restrictions on hosting

images.

CORS AND SSL cert signed by an Amazon approved cert authority must be supported.

```
response.card({

  type: "Standard",

  title: "My Cool Card",  //this is not required for type Simple OR Standard


  text:  "Your ride is on the way to 123 Main
Street!\nEstimated cost for
this ride: $25",

  image: {          //image is optional

   smallImageUrl:
"https://carfu.com/resources/card-images/race-car-small.png",  //One must be
specified

   largeImageUrl:
"https://carfu.com/resources/card-images/race-car-large.png"
```

```
}
```

```
});
```

Error Handling

Exceptions should not be thrown by handler functions. Ideally, errors in handlers should be caught by using try/catch and respond with appropriate output to the user. Exceptions that leak out of handlers will be thrown by default. Exceptions can be handled by generic error handler that can be defined for a Skill. Error handlers cannot be asynchronous.

```
app.error = function(exception, request, response)
{      response.say
("Sorry, something bad happened");
```

```
};
```

Exceptions can be thrown if exceptions are wanted to bubble out to the caller (and potentially crash Express).

```
app.error = function(exception, request, response)
{      console.log(exception);
```

throw exception;

};

Examples
Asynchronous Intent Handler

Intent handlers must return false if they will return a response later. This informs the alexa-app library not to send the response automatically. The handler function must manually call response.send() to finish the response.

```
app.intent('checkStatus', function(request,response) {

  http.get("http://server.com/status.html", function(res)
{
    // This is async and will run after the http call returns
      response.say(res.statusText);
    // Must call send to end the original request
response.send();
  });
  // Return false immediately so alexa-app doesn't send the
response
  return false;   });
```

Conclusion

With seemingly limitless potential, the Amazon Echo is an outstanding device that's leading the way in AI personal assistance and streaming devices. By offering users unique control of their entertainment, daily routines, and home appliances, the Amazon Echo is, in many ways, the perfect interface. With a vast array of feature options and automatic updates, the Amazon Echo really is a premonition of the future of interactive home integration. Amazon has designed a device that not only performs tasks, but learns and advances with the user. The minor limitations of voice-recognition are being ironed out with every update of this device providing possibilities that have only been imagined in science fiction stories. Amazon has now released the Echo Dot, a smaller device that is just as powerful as its forebear.

Digital assistants like Siri, Cortana, and Amazon Echo are

considered closed ecosystems that integrate with selected services only. This limits what can be done with them. However, by opening up the API, other services can easily plug into voice assistants. Ambient computers could compare the options provided by multiple services (such as bus vs. Uber vs. walking) and give the best options by using what it knows about your personal preferences already and use things like your home address and the nearest yoga studio address as data points.

Alexa is always listening, and potentially Alexa could be used to detect much more than just a code word used by a voice it recognizes. Imagine Echo being fully integrated with a smart home, or even being used to overhear breathing patterns and track sleep cycles. When the time comes that a home always knows where people are and what they are doing, things like room-to-room intercomming, with just the utterance of a name, suddenly makes sense.

Ambient computing will make it possible and allow time away from our devices and still allow us all to remain connected. It could keep a database of your interests, mood-analyzing technology, and access to email and social media accounts.

Thank you for reading. I hope you enjoy it. I ask you to leave your honest feedback.

I think next books will also be interesting for you:

Amazon Echo

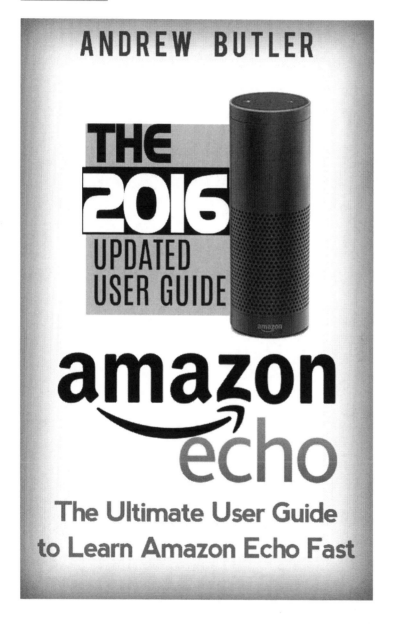

Amazon Fire TV

Windows 10

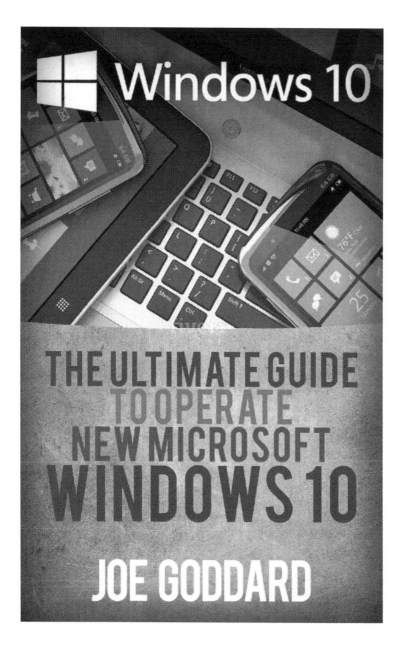

Ham Radio

Ham Radio

The Ultimate Guide to Learn Ham Radio In No Time

Andrew Butler

Amazon Tap

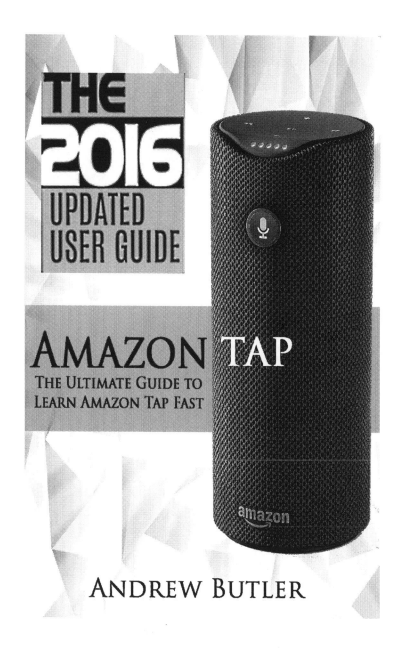

Amazon Dot

Made in the USA
Middletown, DE
02 November 2016